# THE DISTRESSED TABLE

## A PLAY IN ONE ACT

Melville Lovatt

**TSL Drama**

First published in Great Britain in 2018
By TSL Publications, Rickmansworth

Copyright © 2018 Melville Lovatt

ISBN / 978-1-911070-15-3

Image courtesy of :https://pixabay.com/en/table-wine-dinner-restaurant-147314/

The right of Melville Lovatt to be identified as the playwright/author of this work has been asserted by the author in accordance with the UK Copyright, Designs and Patents Act 1988.

All characters and events in this publication, other than those clearly in the public domain, are fictitious and any resemblance to actual persons, living or dead, is purely coincidental.

All rights reserved. No part of this publication may be reproduced, stored in a retrieval system or transmitted, in any form or by any means without the prior written permission of the publisher, nor be otherwise circulated in any form of binding or cover other than that in which it is published and without a similar condition being imposed on the subsequent buyer.

**Rights of performance**

Rights of performance for this play is controlled by TSL Publications (tslbooks.uk/Drama) which issues a performing licence on payment of a fee and subject to a number of conditions (specified on tslbooks.uk/Drama). This play is fully protected under the Copyright Laws of the British Commonwealth of Nations, the United States of America and all countries of the Berne and Universal Copyright Conventions. All rights, including stage, Motion Picture, Radio, Television, Public Reading and Translation into Foreign Languages are strictly reserved. It is an infringement of the Copyright to give any performance or public reading of this play before the fee has been paid and the licence issued. The Royalty Fee is subject to contract and subject to variation at the sole discretion of TSL Publications. In Territories Overseas the fees quoted may not apply. A fee will be quoted on application to TSL Publications.

**Dedication**

Zoe Iggulden

# By Melville Lovatt

## Full Length Plays

| | | | |
|---|---|---|---|
| Small Mercies | Comedy-Drama | 4M | 2F |
| The Powers That Be | Thriller | 3M | 2F |
| Visiting Time | Family Drama | 3M | 2F |
| Desperate Measures | Dark Comedy | 3M | 1F |

## One Act Plays

| | | | |
|---|---|---|---|
| Accommodation | Tragicomedy | 4M | 1F |
| The Lamp | Comedy-Drama | 1M | 1F |
| The Distressed Table | Comedy-Drama | 1M | 1F + Voiceover (F) |
| The Boomerang | Comedy-Drama | 3M | 1Boy + Voiceover (F) |
| Making Adjustments | Comedy-Drama | 1M | 2F |
| The Kiss | Thriller | 2M | 1F |
| The Weekend | Drama | 2M | 1F |
| The Grave | Drama | 2M | |

## Duologue

| | | | |
|---|---|---|---|
| Bedside Story | Drama | 1M | 1F |

## Monologue Collections

| | | | |
|---|---|---|---|
| Standing Alone (16 monologues) | Comedy-Drama | 8M | 8F |

All enquiries to TSL Publications: www.tslbooks.uk

# The Distressed Table

## A play in one act

### Characters

CHRISTINE: *a woman in her late fifties*
BERNARD: *a man in his late fifties*
JAN (voice over only): *a woman in her late fifties*

### Running Time

Between 30 and 35 minutes

# The Distressed Table

was first presented on 7 July 2017
as part of a Scratch Night of New Writing
at Uxbridge Library

with the following cast:
Christine — Esme Tyers
Bernard — Bernard Vic
Jan — Barbara Towell (Voiceover only)

Written & Directed by:
Melville Lovatt

## Scenes

| Scene 1 | The shop. Morning. |
| Scene 2 | The shop. Two days later. Morning. |
| Scene 3 | Churchyard. A week later. Afternoon. |
| Scene 4 | Pub patio. Afternoon. |
| Scene 5 | Boating lake. Afternoon. |
| Scene 6 | The shop. Next day. Morning. |
| Scene 7 | The shop. Next day. Morning. |

## Setting

Four areas.

Small area, stage left, suggests a village churchyard.

A bench towards rear.

Small, flat gravestones, DL.

Stage centre, a medium sized display room belonging to a fairly large, mainly second hand furniture shop. The goods are generally of very mixed quality. The room is used to display smaller furniture. Door and window, CB, looking out onto street.

A round pedestal sales desk with drawer, telephone and two chairs, DR.

On the sales desk, a glass of water and an old framed photograph of BERNARD and wife, JAN, opening the shop many years ago.

A distressed coffee table, SC.

Small area, stage right, suggests pub riverside patio.

Small table, two chairs, upfront. Two glasses of wine on the table.

Small area with two small chairs, upfront, suggests a rowing boat on boating lake.

## Author's Production Note

Please Note: The pacing of *The Distressed Table* is very important and the running time should fall strictly between 30 and 35 minutes.

For One Act Play Festivals and similar events, the central area set can be suggested by the players, leaving only the sales desk, telephone, photograph and chairs visible. The sequence on the rowing boat can also be suggested, the two players, having moved the patio chairs upfront, sitting, facing each other as Bernard rows.

Alternatively, two further small chairs suggesting the boat could be in position from the start.

Ideally, all areas should be pre-set, allowing swift continuity between scenes.

## Scene 1

*Lights Up.*
*Shop. Morning.*

CHRISTINE: (*Wanders around the shop for a while, briefly observing the framed photograph.*
She looks at her watch, sighs, shakes head, growing increasingly impatient.
Calls out.*) Anybody here? Is there anyone here?
(*To herself.*) God. What a shop. Not a salesman in sight.
(*Calls out louder.*) Is there anybody home? Anybody to help?
*Pause.*
Apparently not.
*Pause.*

BERNARD: (*Suddenly appears, wearing cravat with tweed sports jacket. His general manner is a little pompous.*) Good morning.

CHRISTINE: Do you *work* here?

BERNARD: How can I help?

CHRISTINE: I was beginning to think I was here on my own.

BERNARD: I'm afraid ... the thing is ... I *am* on my own. My wife's away on business so there's just ... just me. It's a difficult shop to ... there are three floors, you see. And the phone's never stopped.

CHRISTINE: (*Brisk.*) Yes, well, you're here now.

BERNARD: I would also point out, we don't shadow people, here. We believe in allowing our customers *space*.

CHRISTINE: Well, you've certainly allowed *me* plenty of *space*.

BERNARD: No one likes being shadowed.

CHRISTINE: Even so, I *do* think ...

BERNARD: Some shops are a nightmare. I'm sure you'll agree. Salesmen shadowing. Lurking. Always ready to pounce. Our customers usually thank us for allowing them space.

CHRISTINE: I should *thank* you then, should I?

BERNARD: (*Clears throat, abruptly.*) How can I help?

CHRISTINE: (*Points to coffee table.*) This table.

BERNARD: Ah, yes. A delightful piece.

CHRISTINE: But it's very badly damaged.

BERNARD: Damaged?

CHRISTINE: Well, yes. (*Points to damage.*) On the legs. On the top. There're scratches there. Look. And there're chips and dents there ...

BERNARD: All part of its appeal.

CHRISTINE: I'm sorry?

BERNARD: It's deliberate. It's a process, you see, which is called *distressing*. Allow me to explain. They've *created* the scratches, the chips and the marks. They've scratched it with knives, you see. Lashed it with chains. No violence has been spared to create something ... well ... something old looking. Rustic. Something ... *unique*. The distressing is precisely what gives the piece *charm*. Without it, it wouldn't be unique.

*Pause.*

CHRISTINE: Well, I'd like to order one.

BERNARD: Certainly. Yes.

CHRISTINE: Without all the scratches, the chips and the marks.

BERNARD: Without the distressing?

CHRISTINE: Yes. *Undistressed.*
BERNARD: Undistressed?
CHRISTINE: Is there a problem?
BERNARD: There's no such thing.
CHRISTINE: No such thing?
BERNARD: I'm afraid not.
CHRISTINE: I don't understand ...
BERNARD: Well, these tables, you see, come from Indonesia. They're imported into this country from there. Made by local craftsmen, very proud of their distressing. To ask them to make something *undistressed,* (*Scoffs.*) Well ...
CHRISTINE: But surely to God, if they can make it distressed, they can make it undistressed, can't they? I mean, all I want is a table without all the marks.
BERNARD: (*With finality.*) I'm afraid their contract is only for distressed.
CHRISTINE: So you won't take my order? Is that what you're saying?
BERNARD: I'm afraid there's no point in taking it.
CHRISTINE: (*Losing all patience.*) Well ... I have never heard so much rubbish in my life. (*Smiles sweetly.*) I'm afraid, sir, you are choc full of shit.
BERNARD: *I beg your pardon?* (*Points to door.*) Kindly leave the shop.
CHRISTINE: (*Storming out.*) I'm going. Don't worry. Goodbye!
*She exits, angrily.*
*Blackout.*
*Lights up.*

## Scene 2

*The shop. Morning. Two days later.*
*BERNARD with a notepad, stands, stocktaking.*
*Pause.*
*CHRISTINE enters.*
*BERNARD continues writing, unaware of her presence.*
*Pause.*

> *CHRISTINE clears her throat.*
> *BERNARD turns, sees her.*
> *BERNARD and CHRISTINE stare at each other.*

CHRISTINE: About what happened on Tuesday ... I'm sorry. Okay? I had no right to ... well ... insult you like that. I just lost my temper ... there's really no excuse. Well, I'm sorry. (*Turns to go.*) Now I'd better be off.

BERNARD: Wait. (CHRISTINE *turns to face him.*) I've been thinking about this. For future reference, I spoke to the agent the following day. He says they can make the table *lightly distressed*.

CHRISTINE: What does that mean, exactly?

BERNARD: Allow me to explain. You see, the timber they use is *already* distressed with natural markings, characteristic of the wood. I would simply make sure there's no *extra* distressing. (*Points to table.*) For instance, no chain marks like we have here. No hammer marks. Scratches. No *man made* distressing. Just a natural finish.

CHRISTINE: I see.

> *Pause.*

|              | I came back yesterday. You were closed. |
|---|---|
| BERNARD: | Oh yes. I do close on Wednesdays. |
| CHRISTINE: | Unusual. |
| BERNARD: | Yes. My wife, you see, it was her idea, really. She said closing on Wednesday would break up the week. And it does. She was right. It became our day off. Just became ... (*Softer.*) became our day. |

*Pause.*

| CHRISTINE: | (*Points to photograph.*) This is your wife, I take it? |
|---|---|
| BERNARD: | Yes. An old photograph of us, opening the shop. |
| CHRISTINE: | When was this taken? |
| BERNARD: | Oh, thirty-five years ago. Thirty-five years *today,* as a matter of fact. It's the shop's anniversary. Thirty-five today. |
| CHRISTINE: | You've done well to keep going. |
| BERNARD: | (*With quiet pride.*) No small achievement. No small achievement in this day and age. |

*Pause.*

| CHRISTINE: | (*Stares at the table.*) Lightly distressed? |
|---|---|
| BERNARD: | Just a mark here and there. |
| CHRISTINE: | But how do I know where the marks will fall? |
| BERNARD: | What? |
| CHRISTINE: | I said how do I know ...? |
| BERNARD: | I'm afraid you *can't* know. Natural distressing is random. Unique. |
| CHRISTINE: | Yes, but if you instruct them ... |
| BERNARD: | Instruct them? |
| CHRISTINE: | I mean, instruct the person who is choosing the wood ... |
| BERNARD: | You mean send written instructions to Indonesia? (*Pretends to read instruction sheet.*) Six marks on top and three on each leg. The marks on the top, |

|            | spaced out, two inches. Three right of centre, then two to the left. And not *too tightly grouped* ... |
|---|---|

CHRISTINE: Now you're just being silly.

BERNARD: No, you're being silly. Too silly for words. (*Quite sharp, losing temper.*) How the devil can we know where the marks will fall? I've explained the timber's naturally distressed. It's random. *Random.* Do you understand that?

CHRISTINE: (*Quite shaken.*) I shouldn't have come back here. (*Goes out, quickly.*) Goodbye.

*Blackout.*

## Scene 3

*Lights up.*
*A week later. Sunny afternoon.*
*Village churchyard.*
*CHRISTINE appears, carrying a small vase of flowers and a folding umbrella.*
*She puts the flowers on a grave.*
*She puts down umbrella, rearranging the flowers.*
*She picks up umbrella, stands.*
*Pause.*

CHRISTINE: (*To the grave.*) It's nearly five years. Do you realise that? Already, five years have gone by?

*Pause.*

Do you realise that? No, of course you don't. How could you? You're bloody well dead.

*Pause.*

I haven't met anyone. Anyone else. I've become completely bloody celibate. (*Small chuckle.*) Yes. So celibate, I've almost forgotten what it's like. I'm lonely. Bored. Bored out of my mind. It's not the same, doing the walks we did. It's not the same going for walks on my own. There are days when I don't see anyone at all.

*Pause.*

I'm thinking of getting a dog.

*Pause.*

*She sits on the bench, continues to address the grave.*

(*Suddenly emphatic, angry.*) I refuse to feel guilty. It wasn't my fault. I refuse to accept, the blame, do you hear? Okay, I admit ... I was materialistic. I admit to wanting ... life's finer things. But *I* didn't drive you to it. It was *your* decision. *Your* decision to do what you did. If I'd known, I'd have stopped you. I had no idea ...

*Pause.*

I refuse to feel guilt.

*Pause.*

(*Softer.*) You didn't have to do it. You stupid sod.

*Pause.*

You didn't have to do it.

*Pause.*

I mean, what was the sentence? Three years at the most? With remission for good behaviour, just two. Two years would have flown by in no time at all. Everything passes. *Everything.* Right? We could have gone away, when you came out. Could have gone away somewhere, where nobody knew. (*Emphatic.*) We could have started ... started again. (*Angry, begins to sob.*) We could have made a new start!

*She sobs. The sobbing stops. She quickly wipes her eyes.*

*Pause.*

(*Softly.*) I've got to move on. Five years after all. I'll come again in about six months' time. I've got to move on. Can you understand that?

*Pause.*

I've got to go.

*She once more wipes her eyes.*

*Pause.*

BERNARD *appears.*

BERNARD: Good afternoon.

*(As* CHRISTINE *looks at him.)* Yes, it's me. Me again.

CHRISTINE *stares ahead.*

A small world, isn't it? Very small world. Well, admittedly, this village is smaller than most. One tends to bump into people all the time. That's a good or a bad thing depending on ... well, *(Very awkwardly, nervous chuckle.)* on whether one *wants* to bump into them.

*Pause.*

CHRISTINE *stares straight ahead.*

Another fine day. Not a cloud in the sky. The forecast is good for tomorrow as well. But after tomorrow ... it's not too rosy, then. No, it's not looking good, then.

*Pause.*

Am I right in thinking you're new to the village? It's just that I've never seen you around. That is, before you visited the shop. Am I right in thinking you're new?

*Pause.*

I've lived here all my life. It's very ... peaceful. *(Small chuckle.)* Nothing much happens. Life just carries on. Well, *sometimes* things happen. The occasional drama. The local bank manager killed himself ...

CHRISTINE: *(Looks at him.)* Oh?

BERNARD: Yes, a few years ago. But apart from that ...

CHRISTINE: Did you know him?

BERNARD: Not really. An out-of-towner. Didn't live in the village. He just travelled in. He was caught. Caught fiddling. His hands in the till. Yes, he hanged himself. In prison.

*Pause.*

Look, about last Thursday ... I was rather sharp ...

CHRISTINE: You were rude to me.

BERNARD: Yes, well, I'm sorry if I was.

CHRISTINE: Forget it. We're evens now, aren't we?

*Pause.*

BERNARD: (*Sits next to her.*) Regarding the table, I heard yesterday from the agent ... it's only fair to let you know ...

CHRISTINE: Know what?

BERNARD: Well, the table's been discontinued. I'm afraid they won't be making anymore. The political turmoil in Indonesia ... I'm afraid it's end of story.

*Pause.*

CHRISTINE: So what will you do with the table in the shop?

BERNARD: I suppose I'll just have to sell it off cheap.

CHRISTINE: How cheap?

BERNARD: On clearance.

CHRISTINE: How cheap is that?

BERNARD: (*Shrugs.*) Twenty-five percent reduction?

CHRISTINE: (*Incredulous.*) You call that cheap?

BERNARD: It's a unique table. There's only one left. I shouldn't think I'll have trouble selling it at all.

CHRISTINE: But *clearance* usually means half price at least.

BERNARD: In *some* cases, yes.

CHRISTINE: In *most* cases.

BERNARD: Well ... it depends, of course, on the article in question. The thing is, when we're talking of something *unique* ...

CHRISTINE: You like that word, don't you?

BERNARD: Sorry?

CHRISTINE: *Unique.* it's a favourite word of yours, isn't it?
BERNARD: Well …
CHRISTINE: It's just something I've noticed. You use it a lot.
BERNARD: Yes, well, I'd better be off.
*Pause.*
*He does not move.*
CHRISTINE: It's your day off again, then?
BERNARD: Wednesday. It … yes.
CHRISTINE: Your wife's still away, I take it?
BERNARD: Well, yes. Yes, she's still … still away … on business, she … yes, she's still … still away. On business.
*Pause.*
CHRISTINE: (*Stands.*) Well, *I'd* better be off.
BERNARD: Regarding the table …
CHRISTINE: Not interested, thanks. No, it's *too* distressed.
BERNARD: Yes, well, well perhaps I might … see you around?
CHRISTINE: (*Indifferently.*) I suppose you might. Cheerio.
*She goes off.*
*Pause.*
BERNARD *remains sitting.*
*He produces a folded letter from his jacket. He begins to re-read the letter.*
JAN'S VOICE OVER: Bernard, it's hard to write this letter. I didn't want to write it at all but I must. It's over between us. I think you know this. Whatever we had when we married, it's gone. You say you still love me. I no longer love you. We've changed. Grown apart. I've met someone else. I may now decide to stay out here in Sweden. I'll let you know, soon. For the good times.
Jan.

*Pause.*

BERNARD *begins to sob, very quietly. After some moments, the sobbing stops. He puts letter away, wipes eyes with handkerchief.*

CHRISTINE *re-enters, suddenly.*

CHRISTINE: I forgot my umbrella.

BERNARD: (*Startled.*) Oh ... (*Spots umbrella on bench, hands it to her.*) Oh yes.

CHRISTINE: Thanks.

BERNARD: (*Wipes eyes.*) Hay fever. Plagued with it.

CHRISTINE: Ah.

BERNARD: Every summer without fail, for the past five years.

CHRISTINE: (*Sits next to him, produces hay fever tablets.*) Here, try one of these.

(*Offers tablet.*) They do the trick for me.

BERNARD: (*Takes tablet.*) What are they?

CHRISTINE: Herbal.

BERNARD: Herbal, eh?

CHRISTINE: Right. They're perfectly harmless. No side effects at all. No tiredness. Drowsiness. Nothing like that. Well, go on. Pop it in, then.

BERNARD: I'll ... save it 'til later.

CHRISTINE: Later? Why later? You've hay fever *now*.

BERNARD: Even so ... the thing is ... I'm on medication. I have to be careful what ... what I take.

CHRISTINE: Anybody would think I was offering you poison.

BERNARD: I will ... will take it. Later.

*Pause.*

CHRISTINE: (*Stands, turns to go.*) Right.

BERNARD: Well, thanks. Thanks for the tablet. I am ... am grateful. (*Stands.*) Can I buy you some lunch?

CHRISTINE: (*Stops.*) Lunch?

BERNARD: By the lake? The Prospect pub? They've a new lunchtime menu.

CHRISTINE: I've already eaten.

BERNARD: Oh well, perhaps … perhaps just a drink?

CHRISTINE: I wouldn't mind a drink. It *is* rather hot. And down by the lake it should be quite cool. (*Decidedly.*) Yes, if you insist, you can buy me a drink.

BERNARD: (*Stands.*) A drink by the lake it is, then.

*Blackout.*

*Lights up.*

## Scene 4

*Short time later.*
*The patio of The Prospect pub, overlooking a boating lake.*
*CHRISTINE and BERNARD sit at the table, sipping wine.*

BERNARD: *(Raises glass.)* Cheers.

CHRISTINE: Cheers.

*Pause.*

*They both stare ahead, sipping wine.*

BERNARD: Well, I must say, this is very pleasant. Yes, very pleasant indeed. They do a *good* lunch here.

CHRISTINE: Don't let me stop you.

BERNARD: Perhaps I'll eat later. Later on.

*Pause.*

Yes, I must say, it's very agreeable, here. It's under new management.

CHRISTINE: Oh?

BERNARD: Oh yes. Their prices have risen but it keeps out the riff raff. Keeps out the rowdy element from town. I'm no prude, *(Shaking head.)* but some of the goings on before … under the previous management, *well* … as I say, I'm no prude, but there *are* certain standards. Certain standards of behaviour which must be observed. If we didn't have these standards, where would we be?

CHRISTINE: I'm not sure, exactly. Where *would* we be?

BERNARD: *(Emphatic.)* Well, we'd be in a mess. In one great mess. On a downward spiral, make no mistake. One should *never* allow bad behaviour to triumph.

CHRISTINE: Oh absolutely. I couldn't agree more.

*Pause.*

*They both sip wine, stare ahead.* BERNARD *fidgets, adjusts his cravat.*

BERNARD: Lots of boats on the lake. Never seen so many. I used to be into sailing, myself.

CHRISTINE: On the lake?

BERNARD: Oh no. Oh no. On the sea.

CHRISTINE: (*Impressed.*) On the *sea?*

BERNARD: Proper sailing. The rougher, the better. The Bay of Biscay. Cape of Good Hope. (*Shrugs nonchalantly.*) I suppose you could say I've conquered them all.

CHRISTINE: Weren't you ever seasick?

BERNARD: (*Small chuckle.*) Seasick? No! I was far too busy looking after the boat. The captain has really no time to be sick. Out there on the sea, people's lives are at stake. They depend on the captain to get them home safe.

CHRISTINE: So you were a captain?

BERNARD: On my own boat. On other people's boats, I was part of the crew. Yes, I used to love sailing. The *challenge* of it all. Battling the elements. Mastering the sea ...

*Pause.*

CHRISTINE: When's your wife coming back?

BERNARD: Just depends ...

CHRISTINE: On what?

BERNARD: On how many shows she decides to attend.

CHRISTINE: So she's gone to see shows?

BERNARD: Well ... exhibitions. Furniture exhibitions.

CHRISTINE: Ah.

BERNARD: Scandinavia, mostly. She's hoping to spot one or two new pieces we can sell in the shop.

CHRISTINE: Why didn't you go with her?

BERNARD: How could I go? It would mean completely closing the shop. No, that's out of the question. Quite a busy time of year. Besides, she prefers to go on her own. And it has to be said, she's a much better *eye*.

CHRISTINE: Better eye?

BERNARD: For what sells.

CHRISTINE: I see.

*Pause.*

BERNARD *sips some wine. He dabs his eyes, lightly, with handkerchief.*

Hay fever again?

BERNARD: Afraid so, yes.

CHRISTINE: Better take the tablet I gave you.

BERNARD: Yes.

*Pause.*

BERNARD *swallows tablet with wine. He puts away handkerchief, stares ahead.*

I used to go with her when we were younger. When we first started in business, that is. Yes, I always used to go with her, then. It was different then, of course. Very different. In those days we traded just from a stall ...

*Pause.*

CHRISTINE: We always used to do everything together. My husband and I, that is. *Everything*. Yes. When I think of us now, I think of us walking through the Chess Valley. His favourite walk. When we went there, he said he always found peace.

*Pause.*

I still hear his voice ...

*Pause.*

*Quickly changing subject.*

Well, I must say you've brought me to a charming place, here. But have you noticed the two of them *at it* over there? (*Points.*) Over there by the bushes?

BERNARD: (*Appalled.*) Absolutely disgraceful! (*Stands, indignant.*) I'll damn well report them. In full view too ...

CHRISTINE: Wouldn't say that. You hadn't noticed until I pointed them out. Hello, what's happening now? She's standing up. (*Stands.*) Now she's waving across to us. *Waving* across. (*Pretends to be offended.*) She's pulling up her knickers and waving across!

BERNARD: Outrageous!

CHRISTINE: *He's* waving. He's waving too. They're *both* waving at us.

BERNARD: (*Very indignant.*) Right! That's it! (*Looks around.*) Where's the manager?

CHRISTINE: Too late. Too late. They're going.

BERNARD: I'll report them! Report them!

CHRISTINE: (*Quietly, feigns embarrassment.*) How embarrassing.

BERNARD: Look ... look, I'm sorry. I'm sorry. I don't know what to say ... (*Decidedly.*) I'll report them to the manager.

*He storms off.*

CHRISTINE *starts to giggle.*

*She laughs hysterically, wiping her eyes.*

*After some moments, she spots* BERNARD *returning.*

*She quickly assumes a straight laced pose, staring ahead, 'offended'.*

BERNARD: (*Sits.*) I've reported them to him. He apologised profusely. Very embarrassing. In broad daylight, too ... I wish there was something I could do to make amends.

CHRISTINE: Make amends?

BERNARD: Well, I mean, if I hadn't brought you here, you wouldn't have had to witness all *this*. If I hadn't brought you here ...

CHRISTINE: The point is you did. But, *yes,* if you want to, you *can* make amends.

BERNARD: Tell me how.

CHRISTINE: You could take me out on a boat.

BERNARD: On a boat?

CHRISTINE: On the lake.

BERNARD: You mean ... *hire* a boat?

CHRISTINE: I'll pay for the hire.

BERNARD: No, I'm happy to pay ...

CHRISTINE: Shall we do it, then?

BERNARD: Are ... are you sure about this?

CHRISTINE: Am I *sure?*

BERNARD: You're okay? You're okay in boats?

CHRISTINE: Of course I'm okay. I'll be in your safe hands. In a capable captain's hands.

*Blackout.*

*Lights Up.*

## Scene 5

*Short time later.*

*CHRISTINE and BERNARD in a rowing boat on the lake.*

*BERNARD is rowing, breathing quite heavily, clearly out of condition.*

CHRISTINE: (*Starts to sing, softly.*) Row row row the boat
gently down the stream
merrily merrily merrily merrily
life is but a dream.

*Pause.*

Would you like me to row?

BERNARD: (*Struggling with the oars, breathing heavily.*) No, I'm fine. Fine.

CHRISTINE: If you don't mind me saying, you don't *look* fine. You seem to have gone ... well, gone rather *pale*.

BERNARD: (*Sharp.*) I'm fine. I'm perfectly fine.

*He continues to row.*

CHRISTINE: (*Watches, concerned.*) I have a suggestion. When we get to the bridge, I'll take over the rowing. How about that?

BERNARD: There's really no need. There's no need at all. Everything's under control. (*He continues to row, wheezing, struggling even more.*)

CHRISTINE: When all's said and done, it *was* my idea to hire a boat in the first place. Right? So it's really only fair we should share the rowing.

*Pause.*

Don't you think?

*Pause.*

So we'll stop at the bridge. At the bridge. I insist. I'm quite used to rowing. Once belonged to a club.

BERNARD: (*Sharp.*) I do wish you'd stop fussing. I'm perfectly fine. Look, everything's under ... under control ... everything's under ...

*He is suddenly sick over side of the boat.*

CHRISTINE *grabs the oars.*

CHRISTINE: (*Rowing.*) I think we'd better get back.

*Blackout.*

## Scene 6

*Lights Up.*
*The shop. Next day. Morning.*
*BERNARD stands, opens a letter. He begins to read it.*

JAN'S VOICE OVER : Bernard, it's hard to write this letter. I've thought things over. Decided to stay. It's all for the best. We both know it is. Whatever we had when we married, it's gone. We're different people from who we once were. We're different people. We've grown apart. Changed. Just remember the good times. All the good years together. Remember the good years and try to move on. You'll find someone else, too. It isn't too late. It's never too late. For the good times.

Jan

PS. Please don't worry about the business. The man I've met is *very* well off. I'd just like one thing. The distressed coffee table. I've always had rather a soft spot for that. And I heard, last week, they're not making anymore. So if you've still got it, the table.

*Pause.*

BERNARD *stares straight ahead.*

CHRISTINE: (*Enters, breezily. Without looking at* BERNARD, *glancing around.*) Good morning. How are you feeling? How's the *captain* feeling today?

BERNARD: (*Puts letter away, stands, subdued.*) If you've come here to mock ...

CHRISTINE: I haven't come here to mock.

BERNARD: I'm afraid your tone suggests otherwise.

CHRISTINE: *Look.* I was just passing by and just thought I'd pop in ... just thought I'd pop in to find out how you are.

BERNARD: How I am?

CHRISTINE: After, well ... being ill yesterday.

BERNARD: (*Curt.*) I'm fine. I'm perfectly fine.

*Pause.*

Well, thank you for coming. Was there anything else? Anything else I can help you with?

CHRISTINE: Well ... the table. I'd quite like another look at it.

BERNARD: Certainly. Yes. (*Gestures towards table.*) Feel free.

*Pause.*

CHRISTINE *crouches, examines underside of the table, running her fingers along its edge.*

BERNARD *moves away from* CHRISTINE, *stands, upfront, his back to her, staring ahead.*

CHRISTINE: (*Stands, looks at* BERNARD.) How much do you want for it?

BERNARD: (*Staring ahead.*) Sorry?

CHRISTINE: I said, how much do you want for the table?

*Pause.*

How much do you want? Come on, name a price.

*Pause.*

Just name a price.

*Pause.*

BERNARD: (*Still staring ahead, his back to her.*) I didn't think you wanted it. *Far too distressed.* I'm quoting. You said *it was far too distressed.*

CHRISTINE: (*Irritated.*) I know what I said.

BERNARD: (*Shrugs.*) So you just ... changed your mind?

CHRISTINE: A woman's prerogative.

BERNARD: Ah. Ah, yes. I know all about *that. Prerogative.* Yes. A woman's prerogative. Wonderful phrase.

CHRISTINE: So what's the big deal, then?

BERNARD: Sorry?

CHRISTINE: How much? How much do you want for the table?

*Pause.*

Four hundred. I'll offer you four hundred pounds.

*Pause.*

Four hundred. Agreed?

*Pause.*

Well, what do you say? That's a reasonable price.

*Pause.*

Have we a deal?

*Pause.*

(BERNARD *Still standing with his back to* CHRISTINE, *closes eyes, shakes his head, very slightly.*)

CHRISTINE: (*Assuming 'head shake' means a 'no'.*) Four hundred and twenty. How about that? Four hundred and twenty. *Collected.* Okay? I can take it off your hands anytime you like.

*Pause.*

Well, what do you say?

*Pause.*

Four hundred and fifty. My final offer. Take it or leave it. That's final. That's it. Four hundred and fifty's a very fair price. It's *over* generous. It's fairer than fair. Well, *say something. Anything.* Have we a deal? Have we a deal or not?

*Pause.*

BERNARD: (*Turns to face* CHRISTINE.) I'm afraid the table's no longer for sale.

CHRISTINE: Oh really?

BERNARD: Reserved. It's been put on reserve.

CHRISTINE: Since when?

BERNARD: Since this morning.

CHRISTINE: You might have told me. Instead of letting me look at it again. Instead of playing some sort of game.

BERNARD: I'm playing no game. You asked to look at the table again. I allowed you to.

CHRISTINE: Yes. You allowed me to look at it, knowing it was sold.

BERNARD: It isn't sold.

CHRISTINE: No?

BERNARD: It's been put on reserve. There's a difference.

CHRISTINE: Oh yes. There's a difference alright. And you'll use it to try and increase the price.

BERNARD: (*Firmly, turns away.*) There's nothing more to be said.

BERNARD *stands, his back to* CHRISTINE. *She stares at his back.*

*Pause.*

CHRISTINE: (*Quietly.*) I'm here for two days. Just two days more. Then I may move on somewhere. I'm not sure yet. If it does become available, I'll leave you my card.

*Props up card against photograph on desk.*

Perhaps you could give me a ring.

*She goes out.*

BERNARD *stands a moment. He moves, to the desk, sits slumped.*

*Pause.*

*He takes a bottle of tablets from the drawer. Places the bottle on top of the desk.*

*Pause.*

*He stares at the bottle a moment, pours all the tablets onto the desk.*

*Pause.*

*He stares at the tablets a moment.*

*He swallows one with water, a second, then a third.*

*He is about to continue swallowing more tablets when he stops, having spotted* CHRISTINE*'s card.*

*He picks up the card, sits, staring at it, whilst still holding more tablets in his open hand.*

*Blackout.*

*Lights Up.*

## Scene 7

*The shop. Next morning.*

BERNARD *sitting at the sales desk, writing.*

CHRISTINE: (*Suddenly enters.*) You left me a message. So, here I am. I assume it's to do with the table.

BERNARD: Yes. Yes, it is.

CHRISTINE: We've a deal, then?

BERNARD: (*Gestures towards chair.*) I just felt I owed ... felt I owed you an explanation.

CHRISTINE *sits.*

BERNARD: By the way ... I'm sorry ... I had no idea ... no idea he was ...

CHRISTINE: How...? (*Softly.*) Of course, yes. *The card.*

BERNARD: (*Hands card to her.*) I remembered his name. Just remembered the name ...

CHRISTINE: (*Takes card.*) Five years ago. Time to move on.

*Pause.*

BERNARD: Well, first let me say I consider your offer fair and very reasonable.

CHRISTINE: Yes.

BERNARD: But I can't sell the table.

CHRISTINE: Why ever not?

BERNARD: Well, you see ... my wife wants it.

CHRISTINE: (*Softly, incredulous.*) I don't believe this ...

BERNARD: It's *all* ... all she *does* want. All she does want. I can keep the rest of the business, she says. All she wants is the table.

CHRISTINE: You're ... breaking up?
BERNARD: Well, yes, we're ... breaking up.
*Pause.*
CHRISTINE: I'm sorry.
BERNARD: It's been ... on the cards for a while. The person she's met is very well off. (*Shrugs casually, though very near to tears.*) People fall in love ... they can fall out of love. Life's a lottery. Don't you think?
*Pause.*
CHRISTINE: So what will you do? Retire? Sell the shop?
BERNARD: I thought I would just ... carry on for a while ...
CHRISTINE: On your own?
BERNARD: Soldier on. (*Vaguely, more to himself.*) I might need some help.

A part-time assistant, say two days a week.
CHRISTINE: Only two?
BERNARD: Maybe three.
CHRISTINE: Why not two and a half? Either five mornings or five afternoons?
BERNARD: (*Still more to himself.*) Afternoons would be best.
CHRISTINE: Yes, best for me, too.
*Pause.*
BERNARD: (*Briefly taken aback, looks at her, considers.*) Five afternoons ...

BERNARD *and* CHRISTINE *stare at each other a moment.*

*Small smile from* CHRISTINE.

*Fade.*

www.ingramcontent.com/pod-product-compliance
Lightning Source LLC
Chambersburg PA
CBHW071804040426
42446CB00012B/2699